Britain's Railways in Wartime

Kevin Robertson

An imprint of
Ian Allan Publishing

First published 2008

ISBN 978 0 86093 623 7

Published by Oxford Publishing Co

an imprint of Ian Allan Publishing Ltd, Hersham, Surrey KT12 4RG
Printed in England by Ian Allan Printing Hersham, Surrey KT12 4RG

Code: 0810/B2

Visit the Ian Allan Publishing website at www.ianallanpublishing.com

Introduction

Like many, I have always had a fascination for the Second World War period. As a boy born in the immediate postwar 'baby boom' years, the immediate impression was of some supposed romance associated with war. Only later did I come to appreciate the true horrors that war entailed.

I think that some of this supposed romanticism comes from having been fed a diet of black and white films of the period, with characters such as John Mills and James Robertson Justice playing 'stiff upper lip' types in the 1950s and beyond.

While films made during the war itself were produced for two main purposes, morale and propaganda, their carefully crafted scripts and stoic characters had as much influence years later as had been intended in the 1940s.

Part of the appeal of these films lay in the black and white imagery. Colour is of course a wonderful innovation, but somehow the monochrome images capture the wartime age so well, leaving perhaps a little to the imagination, and yet missing nothing when it comes to portraying the intended meaning.

This is not my first railway book (whether it will be the last is the decision of others!), but the views in this one have had a sobering effect.

The Getty archive contains literally millions of images, not all of which are available to view as file prints and of course many of these are outside the parameters set for this work. Wartime is as popular a subject for the photographer as are disasters and accidents. The wartime files consist of box upon box of views, only a small proportion of which show railway or even transport-related subjects, but those that were found are in the main truly magnificent and have the strength of imagery referred to above and which is often missing in peacetime photographs.

Throughout all the views there is that overwhelming image of 'pulling together', perhaps an appropriate term when dealing with railways,

whilst on the back of many of the prints is the red stamp 'Passed', meaning that they have been passed by the censor.

The images in the pages which follow are in many respects similar to the scripts of the films alluded to above. There are morale-boosting shots of evacuated children smiling and being well taken care of, and also depictions of successful repairs undertaken to keep traffic flowing after the effect of enemy action.

Elsewhere, we see examples of preparation for war work and assistance in its undertaking.

Naturally, what is reproduced in the following pages is the view from the press corps and there are as ever inaccuracies in some of the contemporary caption notes that were recorded on the reverse of the prints.

I may be an enthusiast on railways and perhaps an 'expert' in one or two fields but none of us can ever hope to be experts in all, so a humble apology if I have perpetuated an error concerning your local station, location, or situation. Please tell me of any errors and omissions via the publisher, we will do our best to correct any such inaccuracies in any potential reprint.

I have attempted to divide the photographs into logical themes. The prelude to war, evacuation, preparation for invasion, bomb damage, working on the home front etc etc. Some scenes could also apply in more than one category, but I hope what is portrayed will fit the bill.

There is not coverage of every event and certainly not every location where major work or incidents took place. The scenes very much centre upon London, but this is perhaps inevitable.

It is all too easy nowadays to view the photographs as being representative of a period a long time ago and hardly imaginable to the present generation. Yet, I recall speaking to railwaymen who were in service with the Big Four companies (the Great Western, Southern, London Midland &

Scottish and London & North Eastern Railways) during this period. For them the hours were long and hard and the conditions at times unimaginable.

Of the actual press views seen, who knows how many, if any, were ever used in the magazines and newspapers of the time. In addition to the press photographers, the railway companies themselves were also known to have sent heir own photographers out on location during this period. As a general rule, though, the railway photographers tended to be more clinical in their approach. If an air raid had damaged a coach, then the railway company photographer would show the coach as a 'three-quarter' view, whereas the press photographer would look for a different angle, literally.

For myself, I have never been the world's best photographer behind the lens. Nowadays I admire the work of others as well, I hope, as recognising what I believe will have an appeal.

With the views being recorded by press photographers rather than their railway counterparts, there was little attempt at including the detailed information the latter would have mentioned. Engine numbers and exact mileage locations are often missing and yet I do not think that matters. If you are looking for a volume of facts and dates and figures, this is not it. Neither am I going to enter the debate as to who or what was the most important company or indeed the most versatile locomotive of the period.

As far as locomotives are concerned, to the LNER protagonist this would undoubtedly be the 'V2', but could not the LMS equally refer to the '8F', the GWR the '28xx' type and even the SR with the creations of Mr Bulleid, unreliable, yes, but able to haul prodigious loads. Similarly even the lowliest branch line and wayside yard handled war time traffic, all of which was essential for the nation during this period.

Such the is the genus of the collection that follows. A visual peep into a dark period in history and yet one where we can now see rays of light penetrating even if they were not necessarily apparent at the time.

Kevin Robertson
Hampshire 2008

A delightful view intended to tug at the heart strings and of the child evacuee lost and alone at the station to where she has been removed for safety – no name is given nor it will be noted does she appear to have a label or luggage. Was this then a hastily prepared shot from an earlier period used perhaps to illustrate that evacuees were arriving safely at what were considered to be suitable receptions points?

Below: 'The GWR prepares for gas attacks'. A gas attack was a definite fear during World War 2 and no doubt as an attempt at boosting morale and thus showing how we were prepared for every eventuality, this view was passed by the censor as having an important message to portray. It shows a clerestory-roofed vehicle, reported as having been painted in a mustard colour, and which contained an air lock through which the infected person would enter before passing to a zinc lined room with hot and cold showers. The final room was a dressing room containing fresh clothes in lockers. It was stated units such as these were stationed at a number of strategic points and could be quickly rushed to any required location.

Above: 'Train loads of timber entering London for Blitzed houses.' As with so many wartime views we are not given a location, nor here a date, although clearly it is on the GW main line. The pannier tank has quite a load in tow, no doubt the necessities of wartime meaning also the regulation barrier wagons between the steam locomotive and timber were not being applied – or was this perhaps just a simple shunting operation?

Below: This view of Woolwich Arsenal dates from just after the war when wagons were being built with all haste to assist in moving coal due to what was then the national coal shortage. (The shortage it will be recalled was created by the sale abroad of our best home produced steam coal and being replaced by inferior imported coal and also coal from pits some distance away.) In the background are locomotives destined for export to Hong Kong whilst the huge naval gun had arrived for scrap.

Right: 'Girl Runs a Station – Miss Freda M. Jones, up to three months ago a clerk in a warehouse, and who now runs the station at Pontdolgogh in Mid Wales.' It was stated that 'This was a one-man station although for the duration it will now be a one-woman station'. Miss Jones lived seven miles away in Newtown and despite being on the main line to Aberystwyth there was evidently sufficient time for gardening. The wartime blackout painting on the end of the building and canopy will be noted.

Left: A locomotive shed 'Somewhere in England'. The location could well be Kings Cross Top Shed, although this is guessed just by looking at the two Gresley locomotives in the background. No date is given, although it must be very early on during hostilities. Notice also the metal rod to be used for striking the gongs just hanging down and of course the additional bell — presumably to warn of a gas attack. The gas mask haversack will also be noted as is what is assumed to be a blacked-out rather than just smoke blackened lamp on the corner of the building.

Below: The location for this photograph is what was during the war known as Platform 3 at Eastleigh. The crew of the locomotive are talking to American servicemen. On the reverse of the file print are just a few words: '1944 Troop Train — killed story'. Little, but enough. We know the date, the fact it is near the south coast and also that this was close to D Day. There is also a clue in the last two words written on the back of the print — 'killed story', showing how keen the censor was not to give any clue of a future invasion to the enemy.

A London railwayman with his blacked-out handlamp. Trains still needed to be signalled away during darkness and this was just another example of every precaution being taken to prevent stray light being shown to an enemy aircraft.

Above: Carrying on as usual, well almost as usual. Entitled 'Business in a Railway Carriage', this is an exception to rule where often the photograph carries little information but the caption tells us everything we need to know. 'Since the outbreak of hostilities many businesses have left the London area and have taken up temporary offices in the country, where work is running along smoothly and efficiently. The LNER District managers Office has been evacuated from Liverpool Street to two small stations some miles outside London, and here the work is carried on with a railway coach and a waiting room as headquarters. A sixty-seater railway coach, heated and illuminated by oil, is now used by the clerks as offices, and as there are no inter-office telephones available, the clerks meet on the platform of the station during the running of the business. The girl typists are accommodated in what was formerly a ladies waiting room at this little station and what was at one time the porter's rest room, is now the office of the manager. Employees do not have any difficulty in obtaining their meals, for an exceedingly good lunch can be obtained on board the train for the reasonable price of one shilling. This interesting set of pictures was taken during a visit to the headquarters and shows scenes during a day's work.' The view is dated November 1939.

Right: This view dated 18 December 1941 shows the first time women had been used as permanent way workers on the LNER. Whether the other companies had followed suit by this time is not certain, although all were certainly using women in similar roles later. It was commented they here they were under the control of a male chargehand, although it will be noted it is the women who are carrying the tools and appear seemingly perfectly content in their work as well.

Left: An immediate effect of the declaration of war in September 1939 was the closure of several London Tube stations. This view was taken as early as 5 September 1939 and although no location is given although it can be seen that certain facilities were still available.

Below: A particularly strong image and slightly unusually as the location is also given, Ipswich. The children are there ready to greet their compatriots or maybe even awaiting the arrival of other family members on 3 December 1939.

Right: Air raid damage on the LNER. All we know for certain is the date, September 1940, although students of railway history will note what are articulated coaching sets of the LNER. The twisted metal in the foreground was once a coach bogie.

Above left: This December 1942 picture was made to show men from the LMS Home Guard 'dodging behind engines, goods trucks, signal boxes etc'. Some poetic licence was used in the original caption that accompanied this print, for rather than Brake Van No 750867, the soldier was said to be taking cover under a locomotive!

Above: 'A new English Town for Troops'. The view was taken during a visit to a typical camp town in the Midlands 'which has been constructed almost overnight for the accommodation of troops. ... 1,500 troops, sappers and pioneers, and 300 civilians are employed on the job, including some of the specially-recruited mobile squads of builders who move from place to place. The works comprises concrete roads, sewage, railways and a hospital with 750 beds, and they represent the largest single project of its kind in the country. It entailed among other things the excavation of 250,000 yards of earth, and the laying of 18 miles of road, 33 miles of railway track, 18 miles of water mains and 18 miles of drain. The picture shows railway construction troops who have completed 21½ miles of rail in three months, two years would have been required in peace time.'

Below: Setting the scene. During the 1930s, the Big Four railway companies had been pressing for the 'Fair Deal', which was to be a 'level playing field', whereby railways could be allowed to compete fairly with the ever-increasing threat posed by road transport. Posters associated with the Fair Deal campaign were common at the major London stations, and no doubt the team behind this large image displayed at Waterloo had cut their teeth with the Fair Deal campaign. The Big Four companies worked together as British railways (small 'r') for the Fair Deal campaign and initiatives such as this were supposed to represent all of the companies equally. Here, though, the design of the stylised locomotive bears more than a trace of LMS influence.

Right: The holiday exodus of 1939. Here some of 1,000 employees of Crosse & Blackwell have fun before leaving Paddington for a day outing to Porthcawl, on 17 June 1939. Excursions such as this would later be banned 'for the duration' although there was some relaxation later as government realised the population needed a rest on occasions, although allowing thousands to also wait at a London terminal could also have had terrible consequences should the enemy choose that time for a bombing raid.

Below right: There were a number of major capital projects in progress at the outbreak of war. The electrification of suburban services on the former Great Eastern Railway from Liverpool Street station was one such project, a part of which was a flyover at Ilford of the sort that the electrified lines of the Southern Railway had already used to advantage to ease congestion. Construction of the flyover was well advanced by 18 August 1939, when this photograph was taken. In the end the Shenfield electrification scheme would not be completed until early BR days, in 1949.

Inclement weather conditions were experienced at the end of January 1940, when it was reported that communication between Yorkshire and Lancashire was severed and several trains 'lost' in snow drifts. Here we see some of the 2,000 soldiers sent to help, assisting railwaymen in the digging out of a locomotive on the Woodhead route from Manchester to Sheffield. The catenary posts are already in place for the electrification of this line. As with the Shenfield scheme, the completion of Woodhead electrification would be delayed until long after the war.

Left: Here is one 'railway' whose operations was not affected by the war. The Kenview Model Railway in East Finchley was designed by its owner, Mr Beach, but built by boys under his supervision. The railway occupied a site 70ft by 25ft and had more than 2,000ft of track in both '0' and '00' gauges. The railway was photographed on 30 March 1943, shortly before Sir Murrough J Wilson KBE, Deputy Chairman of the LNER, paid a visit.

Below: Passengers stand outside a closed Stockwell tube station on 6 September 1939. A number of tube stations were closed at the beginning of the war. Some never reopened, even after the cessation of hostilities.

Right: The deep tunnels of the tube lines provided convenient air raid shelters. Londoners are seen here taking shelter on an escalator at an unidentified station during the 1940 bombings. During the Blitz, tube platforms would be home to thousands of people getting a few hours sleep between the last train of the night and the first of the morning. Sadly, the greatest death toll of any incident in London during the war would occur at Bethnal Green Underground station on the yet to be opened eastwards extension of the Central Line, on 3 March 1943. Here 173 people perished when somebody tripped on a crowded escalator as hundreds were descending for a night's shelter, and others could not help themselves from falling too in a chain reaction.

Above: The lull before the storm. With just three weeks to go before war was declared, these men are engaged in loading pit props into wagons at Cardiff Docks, on 11 August 1939.

Above right: Plans for a mass evacuation of children from the cities to the comparative safety of the countryside were in place well before the outbreak of war on 3 September 1939, and thousands of children were moved in the first few days of war. Photographs in the newspapers such as this, taken at Waterloo, no doubt during the first week of September 1939, showing happy children, helped to provide reassurance.

Right: Evacuees arrive at their destination station on the GWR. The GWR Temperance Bar in the background provides further period detail. All the children have their obligatory label, whilst one adult at least seems to be struggling with what no doubt was a rather heavy and bulky suitcase.

Left: A lady policewoman at what is believed to be Waterloo station in June 1940. At this time WPCs spent their whole service dealing with women and children only.

Below left: Not all the evacuations took place at the outset of war. Indeed, after the initial rush, many evacuees returned home after the anticipated bombing raids did not materialise. By June 1940, when this photograph was taken, the 'Phoney War' period of relative tranquillity had finished and the Battle of Britain was underway in the skies over Kent. The notes for this print record the fact that these children are being evacuated, no doubt the bringing of the cricket gear helped take the edge off the situation.

Below: On 13 June 1940 children set off for destinations stated to include Somerset, Devon, Cornwall and Wales. At first thought, it would seem unlikely that Southern stock would work through to Wales, but during wartime all sorts of unusual workings took place, taking unfamiliar stock to many new destinations.

Top left: These children may well be evacuees; here the main point of interest is the paint applied over the glass of the carriage window along the side and bottom as an effort to limit light escaping in blackout conditions.

Above left: Unusually for an agency print, this photograph identifies the location as Plymouth North Road, a station that would later be rebuilt. Presumably the children were destined for rural locations around Plymouth; the city itself suffered heavily from enemy bombing, largely because of its naval dockyard.

Above right: Blackhorse Road, a former Great Eastern Railway station, in August 1939. Evacuation is already underway, the children travelling in LMS carriage stock.

Above: Evacuees leaving Liverpool Street, a view given a location thanks to notes on the rear of the file print in the hand of the late R C Riley. The splendid wood grain finish obtained by the LNER on its coaching stock is evident.

Right: London Transport's railways were involved in the evacuation programme, as well as the Big Four. Here a District Line service has arrived alongside the main line platforms at Ealing Broadway on 2 September 1939, the day before war was declared.

Left: The base of Blackpool Tower can be seen as the Lancashire resort receives its first evacuees in early September 1939. The children had come from St James' School, Stafford. The Billeting Officer is identified by an armband.

Right: On 1 September 1939, Ealing Broadway had seen an exodus of 800 children, bound, as the file notes state, for 'unknown destinations'.

Left: An evacuee rides along a station platform somewhere in Kent perched upon his fellow travellers' cases. Photographs such as this in the newspapers helped put a brave face on what was a traumatic time for children and parents alike.

Right: With shipping at great danger from enemy attack, even when sailing in escorted convoys, every effort was made to ensure that the UK was as self-sufficient in providing its own food as possible. The 'Dig For Victory' campaign saw countless small pieces of land being turned over to food production, and many farms brought out their horses and old ploughs to cultivate small parcels of land which had been left to pasture for years. Production of new agricultural machinery continued, as this photograph illustrates, but there was great pressure right across the country to turn over as much manufacturing capacity as possible to war-related equipment.

Below: A member of the Great Western Railway gas decontamination squad walks through a cloud of gas during an exercise on 10 June 1941. Fortunately, the gas contamination squads, and the gas masks issued to everybody were never required to be used.

Left: Here near Harrow, on 4 March 1940, we see a railway embankment being prepared to grow crops.

Below: With their remarkably fertile soil, the Fens of East Anglia played a crucial part of the expansion of home food production. The Wissington Light Railway, which ran south from the LNER Stoke Ferry branch, with many branches into remote parts of the Fens, saw a great expansion in activity. Built to serve the sugar factory on the banks of the River Wissey, the railway hired in locomotives from the LNER, notably GER tram locomotives normally confined to the Wisbech & Upwell line and dockside tramways, and trains of 100 wagons were worked over the lightly-laid track. An area described as a 6,000-acre wilderness at Feltwell Fen was drained and used for potato growing from late 1940 onwards. By July 1941 it was reported that a field of potatoes planted on 3 May had been harvested just 10 weeks later. Here a Wissington Light Railway train bearing a headboard reflecting the area's importance is seen deep in Feltwell Fen.

Left: A farm removal was often newsworthy even in peacetime. Here, a complete farm takes up the best part of the platform space at an unnamed LNER station before being taken to the West Country.

Above: From 1 February 1940, First Class travel was abolished on the Underground, with the exception of Metropolitan through trains running from Aylesbury over the Great Western & Great Central Joint Railway. Here a First Class label is removed at Ealing Depot.

Right: Various modifications were made to London Underground stock, particularly that running on open stretches of line. Here new reading lights are being fitted to a District Line train, an amber strip being used to deflect the rays of light.

Above: Blackout regulations were relaxed in some areas after the start of 1943. This view shows what appears to be a strip being added to the earlier blackout notice and seemingly being glued to the glass rather than being attached to the notice itself.

Right: This view dates from 11 November 1939 and shows the new 'bright white lighting' approved by the Home Office for certain express services on the Southern Railway. In reality the lighting may have been improved, but the opportunity on crowded trains to find sufficient space for a game such as this would have been limited.

Far right: At some open air stations on the Underground network, hurricane lamps complete with covers were used in late September 1939. Note that posts had already started to be painted white to assist passengers in blackout conditions.

Far left: A cover for a colour light signal is being put in place.

Left: One procedure brought into use in the early part of the war to deal with blackout conditions was the painting of locomotive buffer beams and buffers with white paint. The locomotive was noted as being an LNER tank locomotive and the Head Warden, an engine driver, is seem attending to one of the dimmed lights on the engine on 18 October 1939.

Below: A fogman's 'devil' modified to comply with Air Raid Patrol requirements is seen next to its more ordinary counterpart. No doubt the new type was intended to radiate heat from the metal casing, but lighting it and keeping it going looks to be problematic.

A photograph of fog detonators being set in readiness for the 'big blackout' on 18 November 1939. Photographs such as this, illustrating a normal and relatively insignificant part of railway operation were reassuring in showing that as far as possible, like goes on as normal. Additionally, 'fillers' such as this were useful to the railways in keeping their activities before the public eye at a time when there might be much news of a sensational nature, but which it was deemed sensible not to release at the time.

Shunting at night on the LNER. During the blackout, fatalities on the roads, particularly for pedestrians, increased dramatically, even though there were less cars around. It is likely that a similar trend befell railway staff working in poor light conditions.

Left: 'It's all done by pressing a button' reads the caption for this view dated 6 October 1943, referring to the coaling plant at an unspecified shed. A grimy 'Coronation' class Pacific lurks in the background.

Right: This morale-boosting view is dated 14 March 1944. The file caption states, 'A critical period is now approaching — vast allied armies are assembling in Britain: armies that will soon surge into the attack. Wherever and whenever the great attack is launched, the railways will be asked for a tremendous intense effort, greater than that of before. The men of the iron road will be ready, ready to play their part in storming the fortress of Europe'. An alternative caption was also supplied, reading more prosaically 'Railways at War — Engines on the Ash Pit'. The location is somewhere on the LMS system.

Below: A view showing the day to day work of the railway progressing as normal. Dating from 1942, this picture shows an LMS tunnel gauging vehicle with a platform for workers to reach up towards the tunnel roof as required.

Railway workers themselves were a regular topic for wartime press photographs. This view of 2 October 1944 illustrates an interesting human interest story: 'On the 28th September, Mr Alfred J. Gibson of Wellshouse Road, North Acton, went on duty at Friars Junction Signal Cabin, Acton, for the last time, to complete his 53½ years' service with the GWR. He has worked in the same signal cabin for 42½ years ever since it was constructed in 1902 and many City train passengers today waved him a farewell'. Such interest in the staff operating the line would be unheard of today, and the likelihood of any staff member holding the same post for so long would also be very small.

Left: In the event, this view was not used the print is marked 'Story Killed' on the back. In 1944, staff are going on duty to operate a troop train. The locomotive, clearly a 'King Arthur' carries a 'SPL' indicator disc. As would be expected, no location for this view is given.

Below: Trains such as this were referred to by contemporary caption writers a 'Ghost Trains' because they were never seen by the travelling public. The location is St Johns Wood Tunnel just north of Marylebone on the Great Central main line and the equipment included 'special lights to penetrate smoke'. The train would move slowly with the men checking the condition of the brickwork visually and physically by tapping to detect voids and fragmenting bricks.

Above: Titled 'Two little girls talk to the engine driver and fireman this morning at a London station before the evacuation left for the country', the real interest in this view of 'Lord Nelson' No 854 *Howard of Effingham* is that it shows the blackout curtains, seen behind the fireman. This wartime measure, introduced to smother the considerable glare from a locomotive footplate at night when the firebox door was open, is rarely seen in clear detail.

Right: The work of the LNER clerical department dispersed to stabled carriage stock has already been referred to and with here an example of the 'portable' although for the present 'stabled' office, complete with that essential component of the contemporary office, the ink-well. Notice also what appears to a heater hanging from the ceiling. How long this type of arrangement persisted is not certain, the other companies tending to utilise ground based accommodation, at least for their headquarters staff.

Left: Another shot of day to day life on the railway, dated 7 November 1939. This was taken at Euston during 'rat week' and depicts what was known as the LMS Rat Fighting Squad, which started an intensive campaign in the vicinity of the station. The terrier is crucial to the task in hand — although it must be wondered how it coped with the electrified rails of the DC lines at Euston.

Left: Employees leaving 'the office' somewhere on the LNER, 1 January 1940, after having been evacuated from London. It is not clear whether the 'office' was permanently stationed outside London, or was used to collect staff from the terminus and return them home later.

Below: The old and the new. No date or location is appended to this print, but as it was located within the wartime boxes at the Getty archive, it may be reasonable to assume that the use of horses was being extended at this time in an effort to save fuel.

Wartime engineering work near Park Royal. The notes with this print refer to an extension of the Central Line, although there is also mention of replacement of existing conductor rails.

Left: Bonanza at the Lost Property Office, Euston, 28 December 1943. Amongst the items on view are a turkey and box of oranges, both highly sought after items at this time. The caption notes with the print record the fact that insufficient packing had been used and that address labels had been torn off.

Above: On 3 December a series of special trains was run to Northampton for parents, relatives and friends of evacuees, all of whom are seen on the platform in the winter sun after arrival from London.

Left: During a time of severe fuel shortage, people queue all day to receive their weekly allowance of 56lb coal at Nine Elms goods depot. A variety of conveyances, mainly prams, are used to carry away the precious fuel.

Right: A remarkably powerful image simply entitled 'Spring Sunshine at Liverpool Street'. It is dated 15 April 1942.

Below: Unfortunately some of the views located within the wartime files contain little or no information and the subject matter must then be a matter for conjecture. Such is the case here, although it is tempting to suggest that this may well be an example of staff brought out of retirement to assist with operations.

An ash pit at a locomotive depot in use for LMS Home Guard training, 11 December 1942. 'The sunken track makes and ideal trench...to practise bomb throwing' records the original caption writer.

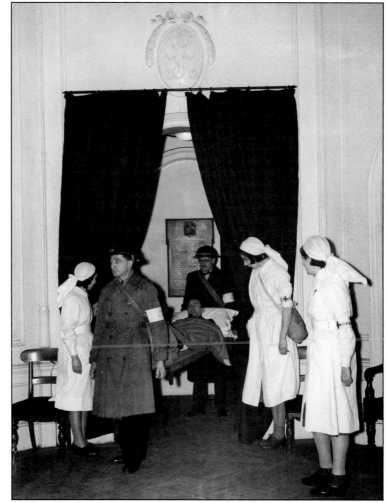

Below: A training exercise in dealing with casualties at Paddington, 24 January 1940. The Royal Waiting Room alongside Platform 1 had been turned into a casualty clearing station. It was reported that the valuable period furniture and mirrors had been replaced by beds, stretchers and other first aid necessities, whilst the nursing staff were trained first aid women from the GWR. Note the crest above the doorway.

Below: Air raid precautions in an LMS goods yard on 1 December 1939. The men with the tin hats are reported to be goods yard staff.

Top left: The Great Western Railway stationed a series of 'cleansing vans' at locations on the system, which could be rushed to any afflicted location. The vehicles, converted from former passenger coaches, were painted a mustard colour and were entered via an air-lock, which led to a decontamination room. A zinc-lined room fitted out with hot and cold showers was provided and after passing through this, personnel entered a dressing room, where supplies of fresh clothing were provided in lockers. A trial of one of these vehicles is seen on 10 December 1941.

Above: A gas demonstration and exercise on the Southern Railway in Kent. Lengths of rail were removed, a crater dug, and mustard gas sprayed. There was then a test of gas detection, decontamination, work to fill in the crater under the same conditions, and finally restoration of signal and telegraph communication. Here the squad is seen cleaning contaminated rails and sleepers.

Left and far left: GWR fire fighters are pictured demonstrating the mobile fire-fighting equipment on 17 March 1941. The GWR set up three mobile fire-fighting trains. Each consisted of a coach for the accommodation of the crew and a specially adapted covered carriage truck which housed two light trailer pumps and other equipment. Both trailer pumps can be seen here, the accommodation vehicle being a former 'Toplight' slip coach.

Below: This LMS fire-fighting train consisted of six locomotive tenders holding 15,000 gallons of water and had several 20hp petrol motor pumps. Another LMS train, designed for use where there was a ready water supply, was of two light pumps, stirrup pumps and 'all the other necessary fire fighting equipment'. It is seen here during a demonstration on 17 February 1941.

Left: The original caption refers to the rerailing of a 'coach' under conditions of gas warfare. The practicalities of working while wearing such protective gear can only be imagined. The location is believed to be somewhere in Kent. The gang will be seen to be using rerailing jacks as well as muscle power.

Above and right: It was not just the effects of enemy action that the railways had to face during wartime. This was the results of the Wembley accident of 13 October 1940. The circumstances were that the 11.50am passenger service from Liverpool was running at 55mph, under clear signal, when it struck a heavily loaded four-wheel luggage barrow which had run down the platform ramp and fallen foul of the Up fast line. The engine, No 5529, and seven passenger coaches were derailed and with nine fatalities including that of both enginemen. In addition there were four serious injuries. The cause was simple, the heavily loaded barrow was being pulled and pushed, one man on the handle and two pushing when the man at the top slipped and the remaining two were unable to hold the weight. This was also the second attempt the men had made to tackle the load up the ramp and had earlier failed. When the barrow did slip the approaching train was only 400yd away and with no time to left to attract the attention of the signalman. Traffic was disrupted for some time afterwards in addition to the damage to stock and permanent way. A water tank at the station was also demolished.

Right: In this view dated 10 February 1941, a London to Southend service has collided with the rear of a passenger train from Norwich, the accident occurring near Brentwood. The Norwich service had been standing on Brentwood bank due to a shortage of steam and was properly protected by a red colour slight signal in the rear. The Norwich service was headed by a 'B17'and which was not steaming well. Under the circumstances the guard should have placed detonators some distance in the rear but he admitted these were placed only 30yd behind, a distance of perhaps just one and a half coach lengths. The Southend service was in charge of a 'B12', the driver of which admitted he missed the indication given by the signals. Sadly the toll was seven fatalities as well as several serious and a number of minor injuries.

Below: There was a serious collision at Ilford on 17 January 1944. This was a rear-end collision, a train from Norwich colliding with the rear of a train from Great Yarmouth. The circumstances were aggravated by darkness and dense fog and while fog signalmen had been called out, they had not yet reached their posts when the accident took place. Nine passengers, including three American servicemen, were killed. The driver of the train from Norwich had missed a succession of signals.

Above: A scene that could almost be the result of bombing but is in fact an accident unrelated to the war. This is Bletchley, with wreckage on the platform as a result of the second part of the Scottish express crashing into the first part at the station on Friday 13 October 1939. Four passengers were killed. This was a case of a driver over-running signals although in this case the train that collided was double headed and the second driver similarly failed to observe the signals correctly. The actual collision occurred between the express and a pilot engine which was at the time attaching a vehicle to rear of the stationary service.

Left and right: The after effects of the massive explosion at Soham on 2 June 1944. The circumstances of this accident have been well documented in words elsewhere, but photographs are rarely seen. These views show the extent of the devastation caused by the exploding wagon load of bombs, as well as the damaged caused to the locomotive, a War Department 2-8-0.

Below: The results of an air raid on the South London lines. The bomb has managed to fall on to a bridge. It was reported that the Royal Engineers and the Pioneer Corps were quickly in attendance.

Right: Whilst this view would appear to be of repairs after bomb damage and indeed it was contained in the World War 2 files at the Getty archive, this photograph dates from just before the war. On 3 August 1939 major works are underway at Worship Street bridge just outside Liverpool Street station. At the time work extending the Central Line eastwards was underway at Liverpool Street, and preparations were being made for the Shenfield electrification.

Some views showing the results of air raids were withheld by the censors for lengthy periods of a year or more. Thus we know the location, St Pancras and the date of release for publication 1941. But we do not know the date of the incident. Apart from the glass, the famous single span roof appears to be almost undamaged.

Right: Bomb damage at Kings Cross in 1941 is seen in this photograph released in 1942. The results of this attack, in the form of roof supports of a different pattern to those of the rest of the train shed and metal sheeting where once there was railway offices, are still very evident in 2008.

Left: The London bombing raids of 7 and 8 September 1940 saw 649 tons of high explosive along with more than 100,000 incendiary devices fall on the capital. The caption to this view refers to trains in a siding being affected, although the location is plainly a station, possibly Liverpool Street.

Right: Air raid damage at Liverpool Street. The photograph has this note appended to it: 'For sale to the LNER only and for retention by them for record purposes only'.

Above left: Another air raid, this time it was stated in South London and in April 1941. Curiously this one was passed for publication immediately and especially when compared with the comments made earlier. No other details were given.

Above: One can do no more than report the caption in its entirety here, on what is clearly LNER stock 'German aircraft again raided this country during the night and a number of bombs were dropped on non-military objectives. Several bombs were dropped on Red Cross trains in the south-east of England, this giving another example of the Nazis and their methods of warfare'. The photograph is dated 6 September 1940.

Three further examples of damage from the raids of
7 and 8 September 1940, the locations are not given.

Right: Air raid damage at York station, which was hit on 30 April 1942. The view was passed to the press on 22 July of that year, but with the proviso that it should not be published until 29 July.

Below: Air raid damage between Folkestone and Dover, 26 August 1940. One female casualty with a slight injury was reported.

The new Waterloo Bridge opened in 1942 as a replacement to the original structure, which dated from 1817. Although not completely finished until 1945, the bridge was a useful link from the outset, with much commercial traffic passing over it in this view taken on 11 August, the opening day. An LNER Scammell Mechanical Horse is to the fore.

Above: Concluding this section on wartime damage, I could not resist three views of the effect on road and tram transport. In the first we see the results of a raid near to Marble Arch on 19th September 1940 and with Portman Street in the background. No details of casualties were given.

Right: A few weeks later on 28th November 1940 it was clear another omnibus had been a victim as staff salvage an indicator blind the following morning.

Left: Finally we see the results of a daylight raid during the morning of 25 October 1940, the trams damaged and at a standstill. Once more, no location is given.

Right: Miss Lulu Harris, who before the war appeared in music hall as a male impersonator was reported in this 28 February 1942 view as 'now playing the same role off stage by doing the job of an LPTB porter'.

IN AIR RAI...

If you are in a train d... ... air raid
or when an Alert is...

Do not leave ... between stations
unless so re... by a railway official
... ck be suspected
... ows and ventilators
... moking
... any outside part of a car

*

IN THE BLACKOUT

Before alighting, make certain the train
has stopped at a platform and that you
alight on the platform side

*

ALWAYS HAVE YOUR
GAS MASK WITH YOU

Above: A group of ladies working on the Southern Railway. A man watches with interest from the footbridge.

Right: A 'Cleaners Parade' at a London Underground depot. These women, whose ages ranged from 21 to 35 had replaced male workers and most of them had husbands serving in the forces. The photograph is dated 17 February 1941.

Britain's Railways in Wartime | **87**

Below: First Class accommodation was downgraded on much of the stock used for the suburban services of the Southern Railway. This meant the removal of the First Class designation from doors and windows, carpets being taken up and arm rests pushed back so as the maximise the seating available. Here two ladies are seen carrying away carpet, while in the background a man is painting out the 'I' symbol. This photograph was dated 7 October 1941.

Right: Women working for the LMS are seen being taught to drive, on 15 February 1943. It was reported that the company had so far trained more than 150 women to 'pilot 3-ton lorries, mechanical horses and platform tractors as well as private cars'. The LMS had four schools for drivers, with students being taught to deal with problems in model form before being taken on to the highway under the supervision of a skilled driver.

Left: Driver and 'van boy', seen on 24 February 1941. This was actually a husband and wife combination, Mr & Mrs William and May Garrard. This picture was just the sort of view intended to shown human interest and how everyone was 'doing their bit'.

Right: A thespian in a new 'role'. Daphne Goodacre, formerly playing the lead in the play 'Ladies in Retirement' was by 18 May 1942 piloting a new 'leading man' though the West End. She was at that time working for the LMS.

Top left: The LMS was clearly in the forefront of publicity during the war for the use of women as railway workers. Here, a group of lady porters, assisted it was said by hundreds of troops, are working on what was described the biggest Christmas freight rush since the start of the war. The photograph, taken at Euston, is dated 21 December 1943.

Above left: A group of women is seen at the LNER Lowestoft works making concrete sleepers. The Southern Railway similarly employed women at its rail works near Southampton. The photograph is dated 8 April 1942.

Above right: A group of 'LNER girls' are seen on 15 April at what is described as a 'goods depot' with a locomotive turntable, which has been raised for a periodic clean up. Rust is about to be brushed off the metalwork prior to repainting.

Right: Here the locomotive *Flying Scotsman*, star of the British Empire Exhibition in 1924, breaker of the 100mph speed barrier and namesake of the prestige Anglo-Scottish train, is seen receiving attention at Kings Cross from Mrs Heward (left) and her daughter Mrs George. Both ladies had husbands in the forces and according to the 'Superintendent' were among his best workers.

Far right: Royal Engineers are seen being taught the maintenance of a steam locomotive. They are pictured drawing a tube from what may well be a 'Lambton' tank.

Far left: Mrs Doris Weigand, 22, of Kentish Town is seen working as a 'knocker up' and delivering papers to the wife of a locomotive crewman. It was reported that she made 10-15 similar calls by cycle every day and at the time, 31 May 1941, she was thought to be the only woman so employed by any of the railway companies.

Left: Inside a Midland Railway-style signalbox. Many women found work in signalboxes.
This view is dated 30 December 1941.

Below: Learning the telegraph on 3 January 1942. The telegraph system was still in general use at this time, the telephone had yet to taken over fully and the era of the teleprinter was still to come.

Right: Cleaning at Paddington, 17 April 1942. The caption acknowledged that the ladies required strong nerves, there being a complete lack of any safety equipment.

Below: Miss Eileen Kirkham hard at work, somewhere in the Birmingham area.

Bottom: These ladies are not undertaking maintenance on the Underground, despite appearances. They are in fact workers going to and from a factory making aircraft components 60ft underground in an incomplete section of the Central Line's eastwards extension. The escalator worked only in the up direction. The photograph is dated 21 August 1943.

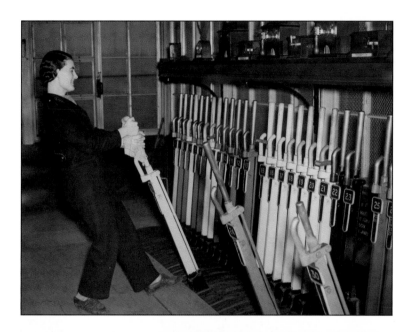

Left: Lady cleaners at work in an London Underground depot. These ladies, photographed on 17 February 1941, had all replaced male workers.

Right: Mrs B Lawrence working at the Neasden depot of London Underground on 11 December 1942.

Left: Inside vehicles of Underground stock on 20 February 1941.

Right: Here main line vehicles receive attention from lady cleaners.

Right: No details were attached to this print, but it would appear to be female track workers at an LNER location. The van, which is probably a departmental vehicle, has a North Eastern Railway look to it, suggesting that this view was taken somewhere on the old NER.

Left: On the Southern at least, the female staff were referred to as 'Pollies'. Here two are employed painting at an unknown location, looking a little disinterested.

Below: Two of the 14 girls then employed at the Southern Railway printing works in Surrey. The works output was some 450,000 tickets per day, each consignment of which was numbered and tied into bundles of either 50 or 200. By the time this photograph was taken, on 6 July 1942, it was noted that economies had even affected ticket printing, as an abbreviated form of the 'Conditions of Issue' was printed on the front of each ticket, which saved printing on the other side.

Above: On a military railway 'somewhere in the Midlands', with American personnel maintaining a Baldwin-built 0-6-0T, numbered WD1252. The railway is believed to be the Bicester Military Railway.

Right: In connection with the early wartime programme of encouraging the nation to grow more food, agricultural tractors were turned out in large numbers at a 'famous motor car works somewhere in England'. These were reported to be the sidings at the factory, possibly at Birmingham. The view is dated 17 October 1939.

Above: Simply entitled 'Railways in wartime, the marshalling yard', this view shows a train of coal passing a deserted station platform.

Right: Vehicles, including ambulances, are assembled on a quayside after disembarkation in 1940.

Above: A train of tank wagons passes Cambridge on 20 December 1943. The passenger station can be seen in the background.

Right: Naval guns are transported by the LNER, prior to use by the fleet, photographed on 10 May 1944.

Left: A train load of
petrol passes through
Cambridge on
29 December 1943.

Left: Waterloo station on 3 August 1940. The caption appended to the file print reads, 'Clearly a sign of the times. Thousands of people usually leave this station in London on August Bank Holiday Saturday, but it was a sign of the times today when this soldier was the only passenger for ten minutes to a popular south coast resort — he was going home on leave.' (In the 1940s, the August bank holiday was the first weekend of the month.)

Above: Ready for action. Mr George Impey, a member of the local Home Guard, is pictured working in his normal job at Charing Cross exchange and information office, 5 January 1942.

Far left: An undated view of military manoeuvres simply entitled 'Somewhere in England'.

Bottom left: From the vast array of uniforms worn, this is a scene that could be taken for wartime and indeed was filed as such. It is in fact a view of Victoria station on 22 May 1937, when a contingent of Australian troops, in Britain for the Coronation, are about to leave London for a tour of the First World War battlefields of France and Germany before returning home.

Left: An unusual load of gas cylinders mounted on road trailers and containing gas for barrage balloons. This photograph was taken at Watford on 20 November 1939.

A group of servicemen at a London terminal, presumably an LMS station as evidenced by the locomotive, in March 1941.

Left: This photograph was taken by Harry Todd, a master of light and shade. A group of British soldiers are pictured at St Pancras station on 22 March 1943.

Above: Entitled, 'Liverpool Street Station' and undated, although the stock would appear to have more of a Southern look about it. Clearly in is from the World War 2 period but no other details are provided.

Below: A London location, undated. Here the servicemen outnumber the civilian passengers. The dog is presumably with the civilians.

Below right: Paddington station. Female servicewomen are photographed carrying their kitbags past a disinterested porter.

Above: Given the caption 'Wartime Terminus', this view of a London station shows columns clearly in need of a repaint. It would be interesting to know what has captured the child's attention.

Right: Men who have returned from Dunkirk wait at a London station on 29 June 1940. While this picture was no doubt intended to show how men and their equipment had been saved, there is something of an air of despondency.

Left: Locomotive for the Continent, 13 March 1945. 'WD' 2-8-0s are ready to be taken to the docks. The note attached to the print refers to the great need to move essential supplies in Europe and although it was clear that the war would shortly be over, there would be no extra trains for holidaymakers this year.

Right: Exports, 1942 style. The crates contain supplies bound for Russia. The scene was at a London yard and is dated 3 March 1942.

Below: This shows rolling stock bound for the British Expeditionary Force in France, 23 May 1940.

Peacetime has returned, but it would be a long time before the signs of war would fade. Here road traffic is having to make a two-mile detour and use part of the King George V Dock in London as repairs to a Blitz-damaged swing bridge on the East Ham to Woolwich road have yet to be completed. It is not recorded how quickly regular passengers on this bus route became tired of their impromptu sightseeing tour . The WD locomotive awaits shipment to Hong Kong, possibly via the SS Waiwera, alongside.

'The last word at Euston'. Three new Lansing Bagnall tractors are seen at the LMS terminus on 26 June 1946.